The Utes

by Allison Lassieur

Consultants:

Betsy Chapoose
Cultural Rights and Protection
Northern Ute Indian Tribe

Terry Knight
NAGPRA/Spiritual Coordinator
Ute Mountain Ute Tribal Council

Bridgestone Books

an imprint of Caps᠎ ne

Mankato, Mir

6

Bridgestone Books are published by Capstone Press
151 Good Counsel Drive, P.O. Box 669, Mankato, Minnesota 56002
http://www.capstone-press.com

Library of Congress Cataloging-in-Publication Data
Lassieur, Allison.
        The Utes/by Allison Lassieur.
        p. cm.—(Native peoples)
        Includes bibliographical references and index.
        Summary: An overview of the past and present lives of the Utes, including their
history, food and clothing, homes and family life, religion, and government.
        ISBN 0-7368-1105-2
        1. Ute Indians—Juvenile literature. [1. Ute Indians. 2. Indians of North America—Utah.
3. Indians of North America—Colorado. 4. Indians of North America—New Mexico.]
I. Title. II. Series.
E99.U8 L37 2002
979.004'9745—dc21   2001004499

Editorial Credits
Erika Mikkelson, editor; Karen Risch, product planning editor; Timothy Halldin, cover and
        interior layout designer; Heidi Meyer, production designer and interior illustrator; Alta
        Schaffer, photo researcher

Photo Credits
Alan G. Nelson/Root Resources, 16
Branson Reynolds, cover, 6, 8, 10, 12, 18, 20
Photo courtesy of the Denver Post, 14

1 2 3 4 5 6 07 06 05 04 03 02

Table of Contents

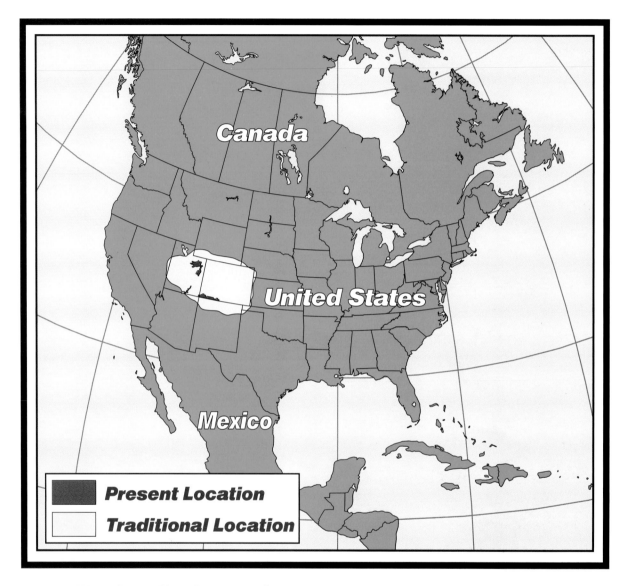

The Utes lived in the Great Basin area of the United States. This area includes Colorado, Utah, northern New Mexico, and southern Wyoming. Today, the Utes live on reservations that cover parts of New Mexico, Colorado, and Utah.

Fast Facts

Long ago, the Utes were one of the most powerful American Indian groups in North America. They lived in an area of North America called the Great Basin. The state of Utah is named after the Ute tribes who lived there. Today, the Utes are divided into three tribes. Each tribe shares a common history.

Homes: Long ago, the Utes lived in small tepees covered with grasses. Later, they covered their tepees with animal hides. Today, they live in modern homes.

Food: The Utes ate a wide variety of foods. They hunted wild game such as buffalo, deer, and elk. They ate fish and water birds such as ducks and geese. Some Ute bands also ate insects and lizards when little food was available.

Clothing: Both men and women wore clothing made of animal skins. Men wore shirts and leggings. Women wore long dresses and leggings.

Language: The Utes spoke Southern Numic. This language belongs to the Numic family of languages. Many American Indian tribes in the Great Basin spoke Numic languages.

Ute History

The Utes were a powerful group long before European settlers came to North America. Ute territory covered more than 79 million square miles (205 million square kilometers). The Utes were divided into many large, powerful bands. Each band had its own leaders. The bands came together if one band needed help or went to war.

In the 1600s, the Utes became one of the first tribes to have horses. They found horses that Spanish explorers had left behind. The Utes became good horse riders. They moved onto the plains where they hunted buffalo.

In 1868, people discovered gold on Ute lands. Settlers then moved into the area. The Utes were pushed off their lands. In 1879, the Utes fought a battle with U.S. officials. The battle was known as the "Meeker Massacre." Chief Ouray helped make peace with the U.S. government. When Chief Ouray died in 1880, the Utes were forced onto a reservation in Utah.

Chief Ouray led the Southern Utes in the mid-1800s.

The Ute People

The Utes call themselves Nünt'z (NOO-chee-oh). This word means "the people." "Ute" means "high land" or "land of the sun." The Utes received the Ute name from early Spanish explorers.

Long ago, the Utes were divided into many bands. They would hunt and gather food in the areas that are now New Mexico, Colorado, and Utah. Today, the bands have joined to form three groups. Together, these groups make up the Confederated Ute Tribes.

The Northern Ute live in northern Utah. This group includes people from the Uncompahgre, White River, and Uintah bands.

The Southern Ute includes people from the Mouache and Capote bands. The Southern Ute live in Colorado.

The Ute Mountain Ute live on a reservation that covers parts of Colorado, New Mexico, and Utah. This area of the United States often is called the Four Corners. People in this group come from the Weeminuche band.

These Ute people are wearing the type of clothes Utes wore in the 1800s.

Homes, Food, and Clothing

Most Utes lived in tepees made with long poles. Long ago, they covered the poles with grasses and reeds. Later, they covered tepees with buffalo hides. Tepees were decorated with pictures.

The food that Utes ate depended on where they lived. Bands that lived in eastern areas hunted game such as deer and elk. Bands that lived in deserts gathered roots, berries, and seeds. Utes also ate buffalo, rabbit, antelope, and moose.

Ute women made clothing from buffalo, deer, and elk hides. Men wore shirts and leggings. Women dressed in long dresses with belts. They also wore leggings under their dresses. Everyone wore moccasins. Men wore feathered headdresses on special occasions. They decorated their faces with yellow and black paint in times of war. Everyone decorated their clothing with elk teeth or porcupine quills.

Some Ute women today still make moccasins and other traditional items.

The Ute Family

Many Ute families lived together in one band. Only people from different bands could marry one another. A couple who married sometimes moved into the woman's band.

Long ago, a pregnant woman had to follow rules before her baby was born. She could not eat the meat of an animal whose spirit power was strong. Her husband could not hunt that animal. They believed the animal's spirit power might harm the baby.

Ute children were welcomed by all families in the band. Older children sometimes took care of the babies. They carried babies in cradleboards on their backs. Other members of the family also cared for the children. Grandparents, aunts, and uncles taught children stories of the Ute culture.

Utes still have strong family ties. A grandparent, niece, or nephew might live with his or her relatives. Family members still pass on customs and stories about the Utes. The family keeps Ute culture alive.

Utes remember their culture by dressing in traditional clothing for fairs and celebrations.

Ute Religion

The Utes believed the world was created by one supreme being called the Creator. They also believed in gods that controlled such things as war, peace, thunder, lightning, and floods. Many years ago, Ute bands included a holy person, or shaman. Shamans were healers. They received the power to heal by talking to spirits of animals and people who had died.

The most important religious ceremony is the Sun Dance. This celebration lasts several days. People from different bands gather for the Sun Dance. Utes pray, fast, and perform secret ceremonies.

Today, the Utes still hold Sun Dances. Many Sun Dance ceremonies are held throughout Ute lands every summer. The biggest Sun Dance occurs in July. The celebration lasts for four days. Before the Sun Dance, Ute men build a special lodge out of brush and trees. The Sun Dance chief leads many special dances. People enjoy a feast at the end of the Sun Dance.

Today, Terry Knight is a religious leader for the Ute Mountain Utes. He is a Sun Dance chief.

Coyote and the Stick People

This Ute story tells how the people of the world were created. Long ago, no people lived in the world. The Creator decided to make people. He filled a large bag with sticks. The Creator's brother Coyote watched him put sticks into the bag. The Creator would not let him look inside the bag.

Coyote found the bag one day when the Creator was away. Coyote peeked inside the bag. The stick people burst out of the bag. Coyote asked them to get back inside. The stick people would not listen. They ran away and scattered all over the world.

When the Creator came back, he saw the empty bag. He was angry. He said, "These people were not ready to come into the world. Now you have caused trouble. The people will fight one another."

The Creator reached into the bag and found a few people. He said, "These people will be known as the Ute. They will be brave. I will put them high in the mountains so they will be close to me."

The Creator sent Coyote to live in the world as punishment for opening the bag. Coyote howls at the sky because he wants to go home.

The Bear Dance

The Bear Dance is an important Ute celebration.
Long ago, the Utes believed bears had magical
powers. The Utes held the Bear Dance in the spring.
This time is when the bears wake up from their
winter hibernation. The Utes believed the Bear
Dance ceremony helped them during the spring
when they would hunt.

In the past, all the Ute bands came together
for the Bear Dance. They built an enclosed area. This
area represented the bear's den. They performed
dances and ceremonies in the area. The Bear Dance
celebration lasted four days and four nights.

Today, the Bear Dance is a yearly social
gathering. Each Ute band holds their own
Bear Dance. The Bear Dance chief in each group
decides when the Bear Dance will take place.
People from other Ute bands attend the dances
and renew friendships with other Utes.

**Each spring, Utes gather to dance and celebrate at
the Bear Dance.**

Ute Government

Long ago, each Ute band had one leader. This leader led the band to good hunting and gathering areas. He also was the leader of the band in times of war.

Today, the Ute groups govern themselves in different ways. The Northern Ute have a business council with six members. The council elects one chairperson. Council members are elected every four years. The business council makes decisions about the Northern Ute.

The Ute Mountain Ute have a seven-member tribal council. The Ute people elect a chairperson. This person holds the office for three years. The business council runs the day-to-day activities of the Ute Mountain Ute.

The Southern Ute also have a tribal council. The council has six members and one chairperson. The tribal council makes decisions about the Southern Utes.

The Ute Mountain Ute tribal offices are located in Towaoc, Colorado.

Hands On: Make Ute Leggings

Long ago, all Utes wore leggings made of light-colored animal skins. The Utes decorated their leggings with colorful beadwork and painted designs. You can make a pair of leggings.

What You Need

Measuring tape
1 yard (.9 meter) of plain white or cream-colored cloth
Fabric paints or markers
Scissors
Fabric glue

What You Do

1. Measure the distance from your knee to your ankle. This number will be the length of your leggings. Then measure around your leg about halfway between your knee and ankle. This number will be the width of your leggings.
2. Draw two rectangles on the cloth using the measurements from step 1. Cut out these rectangles.
3. Cut eight long strips from the remaining cloth. These will be used to tie on the leggings.
4. Glue the end of one strip near the top of the side of the legging. Glue the other strip to the opposite edge. Add two more strips to the bottom part of the cloth. Let the glue dry. Repeat this step for the other legging.
5. Use the markers or paint to decorate the fabric with colorful designs. When they are dry, tie the strips together around your knee and your ankle.

Words to Know

ceremony (SER-eh-moh-nee)—formal actions, words, or music that honor a person, an event, or a higher being

council (KOUN-suhl)—a group of leaders chosen to look after the interests of a community

hibernation (hye-bur-NAY-shun)—a period of deep sleep during the winter

religion (ri-LIJ-uhn)—a set of spiritual beliefs people follow

reservation (rez-er-VAY-shun)—land set aside for use by American Indians

tepee (TEE-pee)—a cone-shaped tent made of long poles covered with grasses or animal skins

tradition (truh-DISH-uhn)—a custom, idea, or belief that is passed on to younger people by older relatives or tribe members

Read More

Flanagan, Alice K. *The Ute.* A True Book. New York: Children's Press, 1998.

Shaughnessy, Diane, and Jack Carpenter. *Chief Ouray: Ute Peacemaker.* Famous Native Americans. Des Moines, Iowa: PowerKids Press, 1997.

Stevens, Janet. *Coyote Steals the Blanket: An Ute Tale.* New York: Holiday House, 1993.

Useful Addresses

Northern Ute Indian Tribe
6358 East Highway 40
Fort Duchesne, UT   84026

Southern Ute Indian Tribe
P.O. Box 737
Ignacio, CO   81137

**Ute Mountain Ute
 Tribal Council**
12500 Ute Mountain Ute 201
Towaoc, CO 81334

Internet Sites

Northern Ute Home Page
http://pine.ubtanet.com/~northernute
The Southern Ute Indian Tribe
http://www.southern-ute.nsn.us
Ute Mountain Ute Tribe
http://www.utemountainute.com

Index